Financially Surviving COVID19
(Deleting Derogatory Credit)

By CARL AGARD

AF810103

BOSS XL MEDIA & THE AGARD FINANCIAL FOUNDATION

Atlanta • New York • Los Angeles

© 2020 Carl Agard. All Rights Reserved.
All rights reserved under International and Pan-African Copyright Conventions. No part of this publication may be reproduced or transmitted in any form or by any means, electronic or mechanical, including photocopy, recording, or information storage and retrieval system, without the written permission of the Author.

Table of Contents

Acknowledgements

This book is dedicated to the 180,000 and counting souls that we have lost so far in 2020 to the Corona Virus or as we know it for short COVID19.

This is a virus that took the world by storm in the beginning of 2020 and changed our lives forever. Many of us have lost a family member, a friend, and/or co-worker. As we try to improve our finances during this pandemic, let's make sure we stay safe and healthy by wearing a mask and maintaining social distancing.

I have a special dedication for my good friend and fraternity brother Jonathan Adewumi who lost his battle to COVID19 in April. May you sleep in peace KING!!!

Introduction

Hop on!! We are about to be on the wildest economic ride of our lives. Not only are we in the midst of the Corona Virus Pandemic that have claimed over 180,000 lives and counting in the United States, we are also in the middle of the worst recession since the Great Depression.

Millions of Americans are currently unemployed because corporations had to cease operations temporarily while their employees “sheltered in place” and quarantined. They have not been back to 100% working capacity yet.

Major industries like restaurants and airlines are heavily impacted because customers are not safe enough to congregate in big numbers as before. The bottom line is to prepare yourself financially for the years ahead with the tools I give you in this book.

Maintaining good credit is always important. You will be able to get a good rate on an auto loan or mortgage. You will be able to borrow money to either start your business or maintain your business. Knowing what’s in your credit report is key; one mistake can cost you thousands of dollars.

I have been a financial expert for over 20 years. I started out in 1998 as the youngest independent Real Estate

Broker in Brooklyn at 27. The next year I became a mortgage broker. I moved to Atlanta in 2001 to relocate New Yorkers to the area and I started building homes for first time homebuyers. Throughout this time I have seen many financial cycles. Some are high, some are low. I experienced the dot-com bubble of 2000, the Terrorist Attacks of 9/11 in 2001, and the Hurricane Katrina in 2005 that affected all of the South.

The worst economic event was the Real Estate market crash of 2007. I had just written 4 best-selling books on Financial Literacy and I was speaking all over the country and on the radio. I was grossing over a million dollars per year for the past ten years up on to that point. Like someone turning off the switch, I was not able to sell a home or fund a mortgage for over a year. I lost all of my savings and had to file bankruptcy.

I had to walk away from projects that I was developing at that time and I had to sell my real estate brokerages and layoff all of my workers.

For the next three years I had to reorganize through my bankruptcy, deal with my IRS issues and I rebranded my business and created a company that funded small business loans and commercial mortgages. Quickly I was back on top again!!

This period was a great learning experience for me because I learned more tips on rebuilding credit, because I had to rebuild mine after my bankruptcy. I learned how to

deal with running a business during a horrible economic time during the Real Estate Market Crash.
Learning how to rebuild and maintain a good credit during the Recession that occurred after the market crash and dealing with the uncertain highs and lows gave me the ability to share my information with you in this e-book.

What's in a Credit Report

A credit report is a record of your credit activities. It lists any credit-card accounts or loans you may have, the balances, and how regularly you make your payments. It also shows if any action has been taken against you because of unpaid bills.

The three major bureaus; Transunion, Equifax, and Experian, collect the information on your credit activities and compile the information on a credit report.

A rating is drawn from the report which outlines your borrowing, charging, and repayment activities. A good rating helps you attain your financial goals and shows lenders that you are a good risk. A poor rating limits your financial goals and shows lenders that you are a credit risk.

Credit bureaus can provide information only to the following requestors:

(1) Creditors who are considering granting or have granted you credit.

(2) Employers considering you for employment, promotion, reassignment, or retention.

(3) Insurers considering you for an insurance policy or reviewing an existing policy.

(4) Government agencies reviewing your financial status or government benefits.

(5) Anyone else with a legitimate business need for the information, such as a potential landlord.

Your credit report is made up of identifying information about you so a lender can evaluate you personally. The four major identifying factors are:

Identifying Information: Your full name, any known aliases, current and previous addresses, social security number, year of birth, current and past employers, and, if applicable, similar information about your spouse.

Credit Information: The accounts you have with banks, retailers, credit-card issuers, utility companies, and other lenders (accounts are listed by type of loan, such as mortgage, student loan, revolving credit, or installment loan; the date you opened the account; your credit limit or the loan amount; any co-signers of the loan; and your payment pattern over the past two years).

Public Record Information: State and county court records on bankruptcy, tax liens, or monetary judgments (some consumer reporting agencies list non-monetary judgments as well).

Recent Inquiries: The names of those who have obtained copies of your credit report within the past year (two years for employment purposes).

Note: It is important to review your credit report for inaccuracies in any of these four identifying factors frequently. Any mistake can adversely affect your credit score. Some common mistakes found in credit reports are:

Misspelled first or last name - This can cause the credit bureau to pick up the information of another person's report. Make sure that your first, last, and even middle name is spelled correctly.

Improper suffix – This is a common mistake among men who are named after their father. Make sure that your credit report has you listed as a Junior or Senior so that you don't get reported as your father or son.

Wrong address – Something this minor can cause a major problem. Imagine if you have a common name like John Smith. If your address is listed wrong, you can be getting negative information for the John Smith at that address.

Wrong credit accounts – Make sure the credit accounts listed on your report are yours; sometimes the bureaus do make mistakes and put other people account information into your report. Also check to see if old accounts are closed and payment history is updated.

Insufficiently reported trade lines – Just as making sure you do not have wrong accounts on your report, you want to make sure that your positive accounts are being reported as well. Check your report to see if all of your accounts are being reported and up to date. You do not want your hard work in maintaining your bills to go unnoticed.

Incorrect Public Records – This is very common on credit reports. Wrong or old tax liens and court judgments are reported by your local state or municipality all the time. You could have paid off your state taxes three years ago and it is still being reported as delinquent. Unfortunately, once the county gets paid, they are not as diligent in updating the status. Incorrect public records are the easiest trade lines to fix on a credit report. Just dispute the item through your bureau, and nine times out of ten, the county will not respond back to your bureau within 30 days.

Unnecessary Inquiries – Too many inquiries on your report can hurt your score. There are several companies that can get access to your report without you knowing about it. Credit card and insurance companies buy lists from other companies with your information on it to send you promotional information about their company; and they pull your credit to see if you are eligible for their program. If several companies are doing this, you can have up to 20 unsolicited inquiries on your report per month!!! Each bureau has a service in which you can opt out of being placed on public lists that are bought by credit card and insurance companies. You can also put a fraud alert on your report so that you are notified anytime someone wants to pull your credit report.

Sort through your credit report with a fine tooth comb so that you can make sure your report is as accurate it can be. Remember, any mistake can impact your score which can affect your interest rate and the amount of credit you can borrow. This can cost you $$$.

The most popular site to quickly obtain a free report that is easy to read is www.creditkarma.com. In the past, there were sites like www.creditchecktotal.com that people used to view and monitor their report, but the monthly fees became annoying and it was sometimes hard to discontinue the service.

Over the past five years Credit Karma became popular because it was a free site and easy to read. Credit Karma will give you your Transunion and Equifax report but you will have to get your Experian report separately. The smart business model that Credit Karma used was that instead of charging subscribers a monthly fee and have the risk of losing some customers every now and then, they charge credit card companies and lenders to have access to millions of potential customers already vetted out by credit score.

This is the reason why Credit Karma is free to subscribers and also the reason why the minute your score goes over a certain level, you get bombarded with credit card and personal loan offers. The credit card and personal loan companies pay Credit Karma millions of dollars per year to have access to these qualified leads.

Credit Karma is now the largest credit monitoring site in the USA. I still suggest that you still set up an account with Experian.com which is an easy to read site and they do have a free monthly access option that you can take, it will just have the fore mentioned ads from credit card and personal loan companies. At this point you will now have access to all three of your credit bureaus for free.

Each bureau updates your report periodically throughout the month from one to three times. This is dependent on getting updated information from your creditors. A lot of times the creditors will update your payment history towards the end of the month so that the bureaus can update your credit score during the first week of the next month.

Tip – To make sure your score is higher the next month if you are planning on getting auto loan or qualifying for a mortgage, make sure you pay down your debt before the 24th of the current month.

Inquiries

As I talked about before, inquiries are where potential creditors, either authorized or not authorized by you, look at your credit profile to see if you are worthy to extend credit to.

When you apply for credit the lender will either do a hard pull or soft pull from either all three credit bureaus or just one.

Each inquiry can stay on your report for up to two years and may not impact your credit score immediately, but many hard pulls in a short period can drop your score a little bit.

A soft pull can be when you look at your own report through one of the services we spoke about already. It can also come from companies you already have a relationship with that wants to see if they want to extend you more credit or a better rate. Soft pulls do not affect your credit score like hard pulls.

Several hard pulls, however, in a short period of time can drop your score from 5 to 10 points within a credit reporting cycle. But in general, the number of hard inquiries on your credit report isn't a major factor in your score. The scoring model is still primarily focused on payment history, credit utilization, total debt, length of credit, and mix of credit.

If you are looking for a mortgage or auto loan, the bureaus will recognize that you may be shopping around for a better rate for a loan and will not penalize you as much as if you pulled your credit for different credit cards and consumer loans.

Tip: You can print out a recent copy of your credit report and let the loan officer review it in advance to avoid a hard pull on your credit. Many times I either have my mortgage and business loan clients send me their recent credit report so I can review it for their score and payment history. From that I can easily determine in advance if they will be qualified for a loan and I also avoided putting a hard pull on their report.

Tip: You can have a credit freeze on your credit profile with each bureau so that no lender or company can get access to your credit without you being contacted first. So for example, if you apply for an auto loan with Satander Bank and they want to do a hard pull on your credit, when they see the note on the bureaus that you have a credit freeze they have to contact you on the phone number supplied and you will personally have to authorize them to have the OK to access your credit profile.

Not only does this avoid unwanted hard pulls, this also protects you from any potential identity theft.

Here is an example of how a credit freeze note looks on Experian. This is what lenders will see before they are able to do a hard pull on your report.

Personal statement(s)

- **06& 08-14-18 0000000 ID FRAUD VICTIM ALERT FRAUDULENT APPLICATIONS MAY BE SUBMITTED IN MY NAME OR MY IDENTITY MAY HAVE BEEN USED WITHOUT MY CONSENT TO FRAUDULENTLY OBTAIN GOODS OR SERVICES. DO NOT EXTEND CREDIT WITHOUT FIRST CONTACTING ME PERSONALLY AND VERIFYING ALL APPLICATION INFORMATION AT DAY 123-456-7899 OR EVENING 987-654-3232 . THIS VICTIM ALERT WILL BE MAINTAINED FOR SEVEN YEARS BEGINNING 08-14-18.**

Tip: You can delete past unwanted inquiries off of your credit report AND quickly boost your score by using the identity theft affidavit and inaccurate dispute letters that I have in the next chapters. I have had credit scores boosted as high as 30 points in as quickly as two weeks with these letters.

Tradelines

Tradelines are an important part of your credit report. Each account of a credit card, automobile loan, or a mortgage makes up a tradeline. On your credit report, each bureau will specify the amount of the account, the length of time it has been open, and if the payments have been made on time.

A bad tradeline, for example, would be a credit card account that has been opened for one year with a $1,000 limit and the cardholder has used up $950 in a short period of time. That would make the tradeline look unfavorable to other lenders.

Another example of a bad tradeline is a credit card holder with an account open for five years with a $5,000 limit in which they have been 30-60 days late on a payment.

A good example of a tradeline is a credit card holder with an account open for seven years with a $5,000 limit in which only $1,000 has been used and $4,000 in available credit. The payments have been on time and never late for the entire seven year period. Imagine having five accounts like these on your credit report. This is what translates you into having an 800+ FICO score.

Note: A method commonly used by individuals to quickly boost their credit score by adding tradelines is becoming an authorized user or AU. A person with not as much credit history is added to an account of a person with a long established timely paid account. The person being added to the account does not have access to the account, just the ability of having the tradeline reported favorably on their credit report.

This has been used by parents who add their college bound kids to their credit card accounts so that their credit profile would be established by the time they graduate. Not only would the college student be able to use the account in case of emergency, they would also resist the temptation of opening a credit account that they would not be able to pay back while in school like I did when I was in college.

There are third party companies who have turned this system into a multi-million dollar business. What they do is recruit individuals with perfect credit and seasoned trade lines which are in good standing, and pay for the usage of the account.

If you want to improve your credit score quickly, you will pay the third party company to add you to the seasoned tradeline. The benefit is that it would look like you have been in an account in good standing for a long time. This will look favorable to a creditor looking at your new credit report, and will boost your score with this new account being reported as well.

The bureaus have been trying to stop recognizing these tradelines, but it is still acceptable because it would negatively affect those families who have been doing this for their college kids and even husbands who do this for their housewives.

Before you look into paying a third party company to add you onto seasoned tradelines, do research to make sure the company is reputable. There are consumers who have lost thousands of dollars paying to be added on seasoned tradelines with the account never getting reported.

What Do Lenders Look for in Your Report?

As someone that have over 20 years' experience as a mortgage broker and lender to small businesses across the country, I get first-hand information from my lender's underwriters as to what they are looking for in a consumer's credit report when they are evaluating an application for a loan. We get this information from these underwriters in real time as this economy is constantly changing, especially with COVID-19. I am giving it to you now in this book.

Lending criteria changed every 3-6 months depending on the state of the economy after the real estate crash of 2008. Banks lost a lot of money on bad loans made prior to 2008 because of loose credit restrictions. For the next 10 years, banks made tougher lending criteria to hedge against these losses whether you were applying for a mortgage or a car loan.

Besides steady income requirements, lenders placed a greater emphasis on your credit report using the scoring models and the algorithms from the three credit bureaus.

With technology, lenders are able to integrate their underwriting models into the credit reporting algorithms to get a quick snapshot as to if you are worthy of a loan. When I first started doing mortgages in the late 90's, underwriting was done manually by looking over a credit report and there were room for errors or an explanation from the applicant if there was an issue on the report.

Now, a lender can run your credit report and decline you in seconds because of this integrated technology. This is why it is important to monitor and understand your credit report and profile.

The top things a lender is looking for in your credit report are:

Length of credit – They want to see how long you have been a responsible paying consumer. If you are 40 years old but only have two years of tradelines reporting, that can be a red flag to that lender.

A lot of times when someone cleans up their credit, they will lose the time on the length of credit because the derogatory tradelines are gone and now any positive accounts that are added is too new. The algorithms of the credit bureaus will pick this up and will give you a lower score.

If you are in your 20's and 30's and have been paying your accounts on time for the past 5-10 years, the credit bureaus will report your score positively.

Tip - For someone that has recently cleaned up their credit and does not have any positive accounts being reported yet, they can look into being added as an authorized user on an account to get their score boosted quickly.

Amount of Debt to Income – After the real estate crash of 2008 the lenders placed an importance on an applicant's income and the ability to pay. Prior to 2008, lending requirements were very lax and in many cases, mortgages and lines of credit were solely based on credit score and not income. When the economy tumbled, most of these loans went into default.

Still fresh from those wounds and now that we are in the middle of a global pandemic, lenders are now prioritizing how much a person makes annually, the amount of debt they are currently carrying, and the stability of the applicant's employment.

For debt, lenders will look at the total amount of monthly housing expenses, credit card payments, loan installment payments, and auto expenses. If an applicant makes $5,000 per month in employment income but currently has $4,000 in total debt, that person would be declined for that loan because they are at 80% of monthly debt obligations relevant to their income.

Lenders now are looking for applicants to be at 50% or less in monthly debt obligations meaning that same applicant making $5,000 per month in income should have less than $2,500 in monthly expenses.

Total utilization of credit cards is very important also because lenders are looking to see if you are 30% or more of your credit limit capacity. So for example, if you have a

Capital One credit card with a $10,000 limit, the lender will look at you negatively if you are over $3,000 in amount owed. Now imagine if you have five cards with close to maxed out capacity.

Credit card utilization impacts your credit score as well in which we will talk about in the next chapter and it is becoming more and more important to lenders and the credit bureaus.

Tip – Before applying for a mortgage, calculate your monthly expenses and divide by your gross monthly income to see if you are 50% or below. I personally believe that you should divide this by your **net** monthly income because you do have taxes and medical deductions that come out of your income. The taxes and deductions vary from state to state. This is money that you don't even touch so this lessens your disposable amount of income.

On the next page is a great personal income and expense report I would use whenever I did credit and budget counseling for a client. Whenever I did seminars, I would advise everyone to fill one out to get a snap shot of what they spend against what they have coming in.

When you write your expenses down and you look at what you are spending, you are able to then cut down on your expenses, from paying down your credit card debt to getting better insurance rates.

FINANCIAL WORKSHEET

MONTLY EXPENSES	MONTLY AMT.	BALANCES
Mortgage Payment		
Property Taxes		
Homeowner's Insurance		
Association Fees		
Other Mortgages		
Automobile Payment		
Other Automobile Loan Payment		
Automobile Insurance		
Gasoline		
Electricity		
Gas		
Water/Sewage		
Garbage		
Telephone		
Cell Phone		
Cable TV		
Credit Cards		
Furniture Loans		
Finance Companies		
Other Loans		
Health Insurance (not deducted)		
Life Insurance (not deducted)		
Taxes (not deducted)		
Donations		
Dues/Memberships		
Medical Bills (not insured)		
Prescription Medications		
Child Care		
Alimony/Child Support		
Tuitions		
Food/Household		
Number of people in the household		
Dry Cleaning		
Uniforms		
Other Expenses		
TOTAL EXPENSES & BALANCES		

Income	Monthly Amt
Net Salary	
Overtime	
Spouse's Net Salary	
Commissions/Tips	
Bonuses	
Interest/Dividends	
Alimony/Child Support	
Disability	
Pension/Retirement	
Rental Property	
Other Income	
TOTAL NET INCOME	

Available Cash	
Checking	
Savings	
Available Credit	
Additional + 30 Days	
401 K	
Total Cash Available	

Total Net Income	
Total Expenses	
Surplus	

I declare under penalty of perjury that this information is true to the best of my knowledge, information and belief and that I realize I waive the right to any return of fee from Manhattan Foreclosure Assistance Corp. should any of this information prove inaccurate or incomplete.

Borrower

Co-Borrower

Date

Payment History within the Past Two Years – When lenders review your report now, they look at how your payment history has been over the past year during the global pandemic. Here, they will see if you were still earning income during the pandemic. Also, they will see if you have to have a mortgage forbearance, a student loan deferment or any type of temporary payment arrangement during this period. This will let the lender know if you had a break in employment during the pandemic. With several layoffs going on across the country, lenders are nervous about extending credit to someone at risk of losing their job.

Generally, lenders will go back as far as two years to see if you have been on time making payments to your creditors. The better the payment history is during this period, the better the chances you have of obtaining a loan.

We all have had a temporary hiccup in life such as a death in the family or a medical illness that may have interrupted you from working and causing you to fall behind in a payment. Some lenders will give you a chance to explain these extenuating circumstances, especially if you were able to get back to making on time payments.

Tip: Scan your credit report to make sure you do not have any late payments reported erroneously. If you do, contact the creditor to update the payment before the next credit reporting cycle.

What's Your Credit Score? – With the Pandemic causing so much uncertainty with the economy, lenders have placed an emphasis on the credit score of an applicant for a mortgage, auto loan, or consumer credit. The bar has been raised and the line has been drawn in the sand. Where 580 was the minimum, lenders are now looking at 640 and above.

It is very important to always monitor and know your credit score so that if it falls below a certain level, you are able to get it up before the next reporting cycle. As we will discuss in the next chapter, the higher your credit score the more you can borrow at the lowest rates.

Understanding Your Credit Score

The first thing you need to know about your credit score is that you don't have one credit score: you have many, and they change all the time.

Credit scores are designed to be a snapshot of your credit picture- typically, the picture that's contained in your credit report. New information is constantly being added to your report, and old information is being deleted. Those changes affect your score.

Because of this, maintaining your credit can sometimes seem be hard work. If you have a bad score now, you're not stuck with it forever. You can do a lot to improve your situation and make yourself more credit-worthy in lender's eyes. When you have a good score, you need to constantly monitor your credit to make sure it stays that way. There are five parts to the FICO Credit Scoring System:

Your payment history (about 35% of a FICO score)
Have you paid your credit accounts on time? Late payments, bankruptcies and other negative items can hurt your credit score. But a rock solid record of on-time payments helps your score.

How much you owe (about 30% of a FICO score)
FICO scores look at the amounts you owe on all your accounts, the number of accounts with balances, and how

much of your available credit you are using. The more you owe compared to your credit limit, the lower your score will be.

Length of credit history (about15% of a FICO score)
A longer credit history will increase your score. However, you can get a high score with a short credit history if the rest of your credit report shows responsible credit management.

New credit (about 10% of a FICO score)
If you have recently applied for or opened new credit accounts, your credit score will weigh this fact against the rest of your credit history. FICO scores distinguish between a search for a single loan and a search for many new credit lines, in part by the length of time over which inquiries occur. If you need a loan, do your rate shopping within a focused period of time, such as 30 days, to avoid lowering your FICO score.

Other factors (about 10% of a FICO score)
Several minor factors can also influence your score. For example, having a mix of credit types on your credit report – credit cards, installment loans such as a mortgage or loan, and personal lines of credit – is normal for people with longer credit histories and can add slightly to their scores.

FICO scores range from 300-850 with most people score in the 600's and 700's (higher FICO scores are better). Lenders buy your FICO score from three national credit reporting agencies (also called credit bureaus): Equifax, Experian and Transunion. In the eyes of most lenders, FICO credit scores above 700 are very good and a sign of good financial health. FICO scores below 600 indicate high risk to lenders and could lead lenders to charge you much higher rates or turn down your credit application. The FICO score has different names at the three major credit bureaus.

Tip: Review your credit scores at least twice a month for any changes. If you subscribe to any of the credit monitoring sites like Credit Karma, you can see if your score increases or decreases during the month. A sudden drop in score may mean a late payment showed up on your report or you may have increased your credit utilization.

Tip: Learn when the credit bureaus update your credit score monthly. For example, if Transunion normally updates your score on the 25th of the month, make your extra payment to your creditor so that it is reported for the next reporting cycle.

Tip: Paying your credit card limits below 30% of utilization will increase your score. If you are not able to pay down your credit limit, try to ask for a credit limit increase. So if you have a credit limit of $1,000 and you have used $900 or 90%, if you request and is granted a credit limit increase to $3,000, now you are at 29% utilization and your score will increase. You have done this without having to spend any money.

Tip: Adding alternative credit can increase your score because it will add more positive tradelines.

We spoke about the advantages of being added as an authorized user or AU earlier in this book. Being added as an AU on an account will add a positive tradeline on your credit report and make it look stronger. But what if you are not able to find someone to add you as an AU? What if you cannot afford to purchase an AU tradeline from a company?

Here are some alternative credit sources that my clients are using now to boost their credit profile.

Secured Credit Card - A secured credit card uses money you place in a security deposit account as collateral. Your credit line is based on your income, your ability to pay, and in most cases, the amount of your security deposit. For example, if you put $1,000 into the deposit account, your available credit line would be $1,000 if you have sufficient income and can demonstrate your ability to pay.

A secured credit card looks and works just like a traditional credit card. That means you can use it for everyday purchases as well as for transactions where cash or debit cards may not be accepted—booking a hotel room in advance, for example. The card won't say "secured," so you can be confident when you use it that no one will know it is a secured card.

A secured credit card will help you reestablish your credit. Making your monthly payments on time is just as crucial with a secured credit card as with a traditional card. Remember, if you default on your payments, the card issuer may keep your deposit.

A popular and pretty good secured card to build credit is Merrick Bank Visa.

Self Lender – Self is a credit-builder loan in which the amount you borrow doesn't come to you right away. Instead, your payments are held in a certificate of deposit, which is insured by the Federal Deposit Insurance Corp. Once you've made all the payments, the money is released to you minus their fees.

Self offers one- and two-year terms, depending on what you want your monthly payment to be. The lowest payment is $25 a month; you can also choose payments of $35, $48 or $150 per month. Self reports your payments to the three major credit bureaus. To avoid any late payments it is wise to have the monthly payments deducted automatically out of your bank account.

Credit-building loans are becoming more and more popular during the pandemic crisis for these two reasons over secured credit cards.

- You don't need money upfront to get the loan, though you do need to be able to afford the monthly payments. With a secured card, you typically have to pay a deposit upfront, and that amount is generally your credit limit.

- You cannot access the money on deposit until the loan is paid off. With a secured card, you can use up to your credit limit anytime — though doing so will increase your credit utilization and hurt your credit until the balance is low again.

Rental Reporting Agencies – If you are not paying a mortgage, nine times out of ten you are renting an apartment or a home. There are now companies allowing renters to have their rental payments included in their credit report. This is great because a large part of your income goes towards paying your rent. You have to be on time to avoid getting evicted, why not take advantage of having this to help boost your credit.

The rental reporting agencies work directly with your landlord to verify their identity and confirm your on-time rent payments over the last 24 months, and in the months to come.

They obtain and verify basic information such as your social security number, date of birth, address, and your landlord's contact information. Your social security number ensures that your rent history is clearly matched with your credit profile. They will then report the information the all three credit bureaus.

A new tradeline is created on your credit report within 5-7 business days. As you continue to pay your rent each month, more information is added to this tradeline. Clients see an average of 30-50 point increase in their credit score in as little as 15 days.

Tip: Disputing and deleting erroneous information on your credit report will increase your credit score within two weeks. From inquiries to negative credit, having this information removed for good will have you in a better position for a loan and a mortgage.

With the tools I will provide to you in this next chapter, I will show you how to get rid of charge offs and collections on your credit report quickly.

How to Quickly Delete Derogatory Credit

A credit report reflects your payment history on your accounts so lenders can see your financial situation. These accounts will stay on your credit report for a set period of time depending on the payment history of the account even after they have been paid and closed off.

If the account is current and being paid on time, it will be reported positively on your report as long as it is open. If the account is closed and has not had a negative history, it will stay on your report or ten years. This will give you a positive factor on your report even though it is closed.

A negative closed account will remain on your credit report for up to seven years. A negative closed account can be an account that had some late payments while the account was open, an account that went into collection, or an account that was charged off. I will go over the difference between a **charged off** and a **collection** account later in this chapter.

A late payment will occur when you have missed a payment on one of your bills. It will get reported to the credit bureaus once you are at least 30 days past the due date. Penalties or late fees can kick in even if you are one day late, some accounts may give you a five day grace period. However, if you bring your account current before the 30 day mark, the late payment will not be reported and it will not hurt your credit report.

Creditors submit the payment history at different times so if you do go over 30 days late on a payment, it may show up a month or two later. Late payments can hurt your credit score depending on your credit profile and how far you fell behind.

A single late payment will lead to a greater score drop if you had excellent credit than if you credit is already poor and you have other late payments. I have seen someone with a 700 credit score drop all the way down to below 600 because of one late payment. I have also seen someone that has a low 500 credit score and several negative accounts make a late payment and the score just goes down a little bit. I guess the bureaus figure they are already at rock bottom.

With today's economy impacted by COVID19, it is easy for someone to fall behind and miss a payment. We are quarantining and sheltering in place so it making it difficult for someone to earn a consistent living. There are currently millions of workers unemployed and several businesses had to close their doors either temporarily or permanently.

Now more than ever it is easy for a responsible person to miss a mortgage, auto, or credit card payment. If you feel this is going to happen, make sure you contact your creditor because a lot of them have hardship options for those affected by COVID19.

Mortgage companies like Wells Fargo and Bank of America are allowing homeowners to skip up to three mortgage payments without reporting any late payments and the amount skipped will be placed at the back of the loan.

The same is being done with auto loans and personal loan companies. They will allow you to skip up to three payments and put them on back of the loan. If you feel you are strapped for cash and it is difficult to make ends meet, contact your creditor to see if they have a special COVID19 hardship options so that you will not have a negative mark on your report.

Note: If you need assistance contacting your creditor or want to know about the most current COVID19 hardship options, you can contact the credit counseling and home retention division at our nonprofit, The Agard Financial Foundation, at www.theagardfinancialfoundation.org or email us at agardfinancialfoundation@gmail.com

After several late payments without resolution over 120 days the account can become a **charged off** account. A charge off is an entry on your credit report that indicates that a creditor, after trying and failing to get you current on your payments, has given up on collecting the debt and closed the account negatively.

Creditors charge off accounts after they have been delinquent for six months. After you have missed the first 30 days payment, your account will move from "Account in

Good Standing" to a "Negative Item". This is when your credit score will drop.

If the creditor decides to charge off the account after 6 months or 180 days, the account will be reflected as a closed charged off account with the remaining balance including late fees and penalties.

The account becomes a **collection** when the creditor sells the charged off account to a third party agency. The amount due will be zero because you will have to pay the collection agency going forward, but the amount charged off will remain on your credit report as negative for seven years unless you dispute the account and get it deleted.

Once the debt is with the third party collection agency, the account will appear at the bottom of your credit report under the "Collections" section and this will be a negative line item.

Popular third party collection agencies are LVNV Funding, Portfolio Recovery, Midland Funding, IC Systems and Enhanced Recovery. I have deleted or settled accounts with all of them.

These collection agencies are very aggressive and now you will have to settle the debt with them instead of the original creditor because they have bought the debt. The good thing about it is that they are easy to delete off of your credit report because they input several mistakes on your account when they report it to the bureaus and they also do not respond from request for information from the bureaus within 30 days.

Removing a negatively closed account can be difficult, but I will give you the tools to do it quickly and effectively.

You can file a dispute with the three credit bureaus by mail and through their websites. I advise to do both methods and make sure it is consistent. By law, when you dispute an inaccuracy on your credit report, the creditor has to respond within 30 days or the account either has to be deleted for good off of your credit report or updated. Your main objective is to get the negative account that you disputed to be deleted so that this will increase your score and make your credit profile look better.

First, review your negative account for any errors or anything that is inaccurate. It can be an incorrect account number, your name misspelled, or the dates of payment were not entered correctly. These mistakes will enable the three bureaus to notify the creditor to validate this error within 30 days or the bureau will take it off of your credit report.

Here is the address to file a dispute with the three credit bureaus through the mail and also their website.

Transunion
P.O. Box 2000
Chester, PA 19016
www.transunion.com/dispute

800-916-8800

Equifax
P.O. Box 740256
Atlanta, GA 30374
www.myequifax.com
866-349-5191

Experian
P.O. Box 9701
Allen, TX 75013
www.experian.com/dispute
888-397-3742

Electronically you can go to the dispute center on the bureaus' website once you have opened your account and you pulled up your credit report.

You can open up an investigation there for free. You will be able to find the negative accounts and click it. For example purposes, let's say that you have a late payment with Ally Auto Loans, a charge off with Sears, and a collection with IC Systems. You want to dispute all three of these accounts with each bureau both online and in the mail because you want to improve your score and these are old accounts.

You can identify the three negative accounts and select from the drop down menu "not my account and/or inaccurate" or if you have been a victim of identity theft you can select that drop down.

Make sure you do this with all three bureaus online so that your reports will be lined up and matching. When you submit the dispute electronically they will give you an investigation case number.

Tip: I suggest that you dispute all inquiries as well so that they will get deleted and boost your score. Select either "Not Authorized" or "Identity Theft" in the drop down menu.

Ally Auto, Sears, and IC Systems will be notified by the bureaus and they will have 30 days to respond to the investigation or the account will be deleted off of your credit report.

Tip: Make sure you check your email and physical mail for correspondences from the credit bureaus during the course of the month. They may want you to either answer questions or provide any supporting information on these accounts. Any missed correspondences may delay your investigation or the account may get validated and remain on your report.

Send by certify mail a physical dispute form to each bureau to the addresses I gave you in the previous page. You must send your forms and letters by certified mail to have a record that you sent in your dispute.

You can send a letter that the accounts are inaccurate and not reported correctly. Do one letter for each account so for this example you will send three letters to each bureau. You want to list the name of the account, and why it is inaccurate. Keep it simple and say that it is not your account. You must include a copy of your photo ID; such as a driver's license or passport, a copy of your social security card, and a current utility bill of your current address.

Your letter should clearly identify each item in your report you dispute, state the facts and explain why you dispute the information, and request that it be removed or corrected. You may want to enclose a copy of your report with the items in question circled.

Send your letter by certified mail, "return receipt requested," so you can document what the credit reporting company received.

Remember to include copies of the applicable enclosures and save copies for your files. Here's a couple of sample letters that you can use on the next page.

[Your Name]
[Your Address]
[Your City, State, Zip Code]
[Date]

Complaint Department
[Company Name]
[Street Address]
[City, State, Zip Code]

Dear Sir or Madam:

I am writing to dispute the following information in my file. I have circled the items I dispute on the attached copy of the report I received.

This item **[identify item(s) disputed by name of source, such as creditors or tax court, and identify type of item, such as credit account, judgment, etc.]** is **[inaccurate or incomplete]** because **[describe what is inaccurate or incomplete and why]**. I am requesting that the item be removed **[or request another specific change]** to correct the information.

Enclosed are copies of **[use this sentence if applicable and describe any enclosed documentation, such as payment records and court documents]** supporting my position. Please reinvestigate this **[these]** matter**[s]** and **[delete or correct]** the disputed item**[s]** as soon as possible.

Sincerely,

Your name

Enclosures: **[List what you are enclosing.]**

[Date]

[Your Name]

[Your Address]
[Your City, State, Zip Code]
[Name of Credit Bureau]
[Address]
[City, State, Zip Code]
Dear Sir/Ma'am:

I am writing to dispute the following information in my file:
Item 1: Name of Source, Type of Item, Account Number or Identifier

Item 2 if required,

You will also find this item circled on the attached credit report. The item I have identified is inaccurate/incomplete because [reason for the issue including any supporting facts/evidence].
I am requesting that this item be deleted in order adequately reflect my true credit history on the attached report.
I have attached all necessary supporting documentation to support my claim.

I am asking you to reexamine this item and remove it from my file at your earliest convenience. I sent this letter via certified mail to ensure this matter is resolved within the required 30-day window.
Sincerely,

Your name

Enclosures: List any included files / attachments

With the rise of anonymous identity theft because of hacker's ability to access our credit profile, you can also submit an identity theft affidavit to each bureau. This is very effective in deleting items off of your credit report.

Millions of consumer's credit profiles are compromised every year. The hackers can access your profile either through your computer or a larger corporation's system. This is why I advocate checking your credit report on Credit Karma monthly.

You can submit an identity theft affidavit and state that your credit profile was compromised within the past two years and dispute the negative accounts and inquiries. You must state that you cannot provide a police report because you was hacked anonymously and do not know who compromised your report.

You will have to provide copies of your photo ID, social security card, and current utility bill. Have the affidavit notarized and send by certified mail to each credit bureau.

Disputing electronically and mailing in letters and affidavits at the same time is very effective in deleting derogatory accounts off of your credit. I have seen results as quick as two weeks.

You can request the latest identity theft affidavit on our website www.theagardfinancialfoundation.org we also provide step by step assistance in filling out the form.

When the investigation is complete, the credit reporting company must give you the results in writing and a free copy of your report if the dispute results in a change. This free report does not count as your annual free report.

If an item is changed or deleted, the credit reporting company cannot put the disputed information back in your file unless the information provider verifies that it is accurate and complete. The credit reporting company also must send you written notice that includes the name, address, and phone number of the information provider.

From our example, you have a good chance of the Ally auto payment lates, the Sear's charge off, and the IC Systems collections deleted. If any of the creditors validate the account and verify it is accurate, you are able to do an appeal. Persistence is important because you may be able to get the items deleted on the second or third round.

But what if there is an account that is validated and you cannot get the item deleted off of your account? In the next chapter I will go over how to settle a charge off or collection account for pennies on the dollar.

How to Settle Charge Offs and Collections

If a charge off or collection is validated and stays on your credit report, all is not lost. You can contact that creditor and settle the account for far less than what you owe and have it deleted.

You want to deal with it and do not ignore it because having an active charge off does not look good on your credit report.

Why would a creditor do this? For them, something is better than nothing. Whatever the creditor can get is better than them having to write off the debt and get nothing.

When they do write off the debt, they sell it to a third party collection agency for a fraction of that debt. You can negotiate a settlement for deletion with a collection agency as well. They bought the debt for a fraction of what you owed, so they have room to settle the account with you.

In both cases it is imperative to get the settlement in writing.

You want to convince the creditor to remove the charge-off from your credit report in exchange for payment. Before you make the call, know how much you're able to pay on the account. The more you can pay and the sooner you can pay it, the more negotiating power you have. However,

I always suggest starting at 20% of what you owe. So if you have a charge off or collection account for $1,000, start with an offer of $200.

I've had cases where the creditor took the settlement amount and paid off the account and got it deleted off of the credit report. There will be some cases where they will counter with a higher offer so that's why I like to start with 20%. If the creditor counters back at 50% or $500, you still settled the account for far less than what you owe. Initially offering 20% gives you that wiggle room.

Send your offer in writing so that you have a record of the conversation especially if they agree on a settlement. If you do not have it in writing, someone else at the creditor may come back and say the settlement never existed. If they do not agree on a "pay for deletion", ask for a "paid as closed" settlement.

Besides having your offer in writing, get the final settlement from the creditor in writing with the amount to pay, payment instructions, and any other agreements like if they will delete the account or state it as just closed, and that they do not go after you for any future amounts.

Here is an example of a pay for deletion letter you can use on the next page.

Your Name
Your Address Your City, State Zip
Collector's Name
Collector's Address
Collector's City, State Zip
Date
Re: Account Number XXXX-XXXX-XXXX-XXXX

I am willing to pay **[this debt in full / $XXX as settlement for this debt]** in return for your agreement to remove all information regarding this debt from the credit reporting agencies within ten calendar days of payment. If you agree to the terms, I will send certified payment in the amount of **$XXX** payable to **[Collection Agency]** in exchange to have all information related to this debt removed from all of my credit files.

Please forward your agreement to the address listed above.

Sincerely,

Your Name

Tip: Make sure the collection agency has the rights to collect on the debt. Many times collection debts are bought, sold and transferred to different companies. You do not want to send the wrong company your money.

Tip: If you are negotiating a charged off account, make sure the creditor hasn't sold the debt to a third party collection agency yet and that the original creditor still have the rights to settle the debt.

Tip: Do not be afraid to offer 20%. You may owe an exorbitant amount for a long period of time but you would be surprised what these creditors will accept to close out a bad debt.

Tip: After you settled and closed the account, check your credit to see how they reported the account on your next credit report. You want to see if the creditor deleted the account, the bureaus deleted the account, or if they moved it to "paid and closed" status.

You can still dispute the account as inaccurate and because it is a closed account, the creditor may not reply and you have a great chance of having the account not showing up at all in the future.

Tip: Keep your offer letter and the settlement letter in your files. If the account is not being reported accurately, you have your records to send to the bureau to get it deleted.

On the next page is an example of a "paid and closed" settlement letter from one of my clients.

Dear Member:

This letter confirms the settlement agreement for the above-referenced account.

Navy Federal Credit Union agrees to accept a settlement amount of $5,500.00. We agree to an installment plan consisting of 1 lump sum payments of $5,500.00 each, with the final payment to be received no later than 09/30/2020. The outstanding default will continue to be reported to the credit bureaus until the agreement is satisfied, at which time we will update the credit bureaus with the new information.

By remitting payments in the amount and as outlined above, you are confirming your agreement to settle this account. Upon completion of the settlement, Navy Federal will send you a letter confirming the settlement of the account for your records, an update will be sent to the major credit bureaus that the account has been settled, and no further collection activities will occur.

Sincerely,

Collections Department Navy Federal Credit Union

Enclosures:
Loan Payment Voucher Return Envelope

Where Do We Go From Here??

As we prepare for life after the COVID19 Pandemic one thing we know that there is a lot of uncertainty. A lot depends on a cure or vaccination. We do not know if life as we knew it will ever come back again.

The economy will be unstable for years to come because it will take time for people to get back to the new normal of work, play and school. No matter what, it will still be important to stay ahead of your finances. Budgeting is going to be just as important as keeping your credit score good.

Make sure you save money and make wise investments. Look into stocks and real estate because they will be at a good price during a down economy. For real estate you need to follow the tips in this book so that you can secure a good mortgage. Rates are at an all-time low right now.

If you need any assistance in boosting your credit score, deleting derogatory accounts, or settling charge offs and collections, contact us through our website
www.theagardfinancialfoundation.org
email – agardfinancialfoundation@gmail.com

Glossary

Authorized User
A person who is sharing a credit card and has the right to use it, but does not have responsibility for payment

Business Credit Report
A business credit report is a report showing the credit worthiness of a company. In the United States, the two main providers of business credit reports are Dunn & Bradstreet, and Experian. Most business credit information is not subject to the Fair Credit Reporting Act.

Charge off
A charge-off occurs when a creditor decides that a debt is unlikely to be repaid, and considers it a loss for accounting purposes.

Consumer Reporting Agency
A consumer reporting agency is a company that gathers and stores personal credit histories, and provides credit reports upon request to its customers. The three main credit reporting agencies (CRA's) are Equifax, Experian, and Trans Union. Credit reporting agencies are subject to the Fair Credit Reporting Act, and they take care to ensure that their customers are legitimate businesses and financial institutions having a permissible purpose to request credit reports.

Consumer Statement
If a dispute over a credit report item is not resolved to the consumer's satisfaction, a short message can be added to the credit report to express the consumer's disagreement with the reported item.

Credit Bureau
A credit bureau is a company (or, sometimes, an organization of local merchants) that provides credit reports to its members. Most towns once had their own local credit bureaus. The records were kept manually, and the credit reports were often done verbally. Over the past 20 years, most local credit bureaus have been acquired by Experian, Equifax, and Trans Union. Those who remain independent, in most cases, have an affiliation with one of the three nationwide bureaus. The term credit bureau, as commonly used, refers to any of these organizations.

Credit report
A report designed to indicate your existing debts and how well you've repaid past debts. It also lists the companies that have inquired about your credit recently, and public records such as bankruptcies, judgments, and foreclosures. To the extent provided by your creditors and other sources, your credit report also includes current and prior addresses, current and prior employment, and identification information such as date of birth, driver's license number, and social security number.

Credit Score
A computerized evaluation of your credit worthiness, expressed as a number. A credit score is based on the contents of your Equifax, Experian, or Trans Union credit report. A credit scoring model adds and subtracts points based on factors such as how many and what types of accounts you have, how close you are to your credit limits, how many times you've been late, severity of your delinquencies, and recent levels of activity in applying for credit. Lenders establish their own "cut-off" points for good scores vs. bad, and they may factor-in non-credit report items, such as income and bank balance.

Creditor
A creditor is someone who has loaned money to another. Opposite of debtor.

Debtor
A debtor is someone who has borrowed money from another. Opposite of creditor.

Derogatory
Negative information on a credit report.

Equifax
Equifax is one of the three nationwide credit reporting companies. It is headquartered in Atlanta, Georgia, and employs 5,000 people in 13 countries, with $1.1 billion in annual sales.

Experian
Experian is one of the three nationwide credit reporting companies, created in 1996 when TRW sold-off its credit reporting business. Headquartered in Allen, Texas. Employs more than 12,000 people, and has annual sales of $1.5 billion.

Fair Credit Reporting Act
The Fair Credit Reporting Act (FCRA) is a law that governs credit reporting agencies and establishes consumer rights involving credit reports. The FCRA limits the purposes for which credit information can be provided, and ensures that consumers have rights (for free or at a nominal charge) to see what's in their own credit file. Consumers also have the right to get erroneous items removed.

FICO
A credit score that is computed from an Experian credit report, based on scoring models developed by Experian and Fair, Isaac and Company, Inc.

Fraud Alert
In the event of identity theft or fraud, a security freeze is a temporary hold on your credit report, preventing new credit grantors from seeing it (until you release the freeze.) Court orders, child support enforcement, and companies with which you already have a credit relationship are not subjected to the freeze.

FTC
The Federal Trade Commission (FTC) is the U.S.

Government agency most responsible for regulating the credit reporting agencies. It is also maintains a national database of identity theft complaints, and is active in educating consumers

Hard Inquiry
An inquiry made by a creditor or lender with whom you have applied for credit or a loan. Hard inquiries (up to 2 years old) are part of the report that creditors and lenders see when you apply for new credit, and they are used in the computation of your credit score.

Inquiry
An inquiry is an instance in which a credit report has been requested and viewed. All inquiries are logged by the credit reporting agency. Credit grantors (such as lenders and landlords) can see which other credit grantors have inquired over the last two years. In a consumer disclosure you can see all inquiries, including those hidden to credit grantors.

Instant Update
Instant Update is a capability for a subscriber to quickly add derogatory information to a person's credit report, without waiting for the normal monthly update. For example, after an automobile repossession, an instant update might prevent the consumer from quickly buying another car on credit.

Identity Theft
A crime in which an impostor uses the name, social

security number, and/or other identifying information of a victim to open credit accounts, use existing credit accounts, or otherwise acquire benefits using the victim's identity. Identity thieves sometimes change the address and phone number on a victim's accounts, ruining their credit before the theft has been discovered. A credit report is often the best way to discover identity theft, and a security alert on one's credit report is often the best way to prevent further occurrences when fraud has been discovered.

Investigation
An investigation is the process followed when a consumer submits a dispute to the credit bureau. The bureau refers the questioned item back to the original information provider for verification.

Joint Account
An account in which two people share full responsibility for repayment.

Public Record
Court judgments, foreclosures, and bankruptcies are shown in the public records part of a credit report. Companies and individuals that don't have a relationship with a credit bureau or collection agency cannot get negative information added to your credit report, other than by getting a court judgment against you. Credit bureaus automatically include information gathered from the courts.

Soft Inquiry

An inquiry that is recorded when you request your own credit report, or when your employer requests it. Soft inquiries are not revealed to creditors and lenders, and they do not affect your credit score. Security Alert In the event of identity theft or fraud, you may request that a message be placed on your credit report. The message indicates that you are a possible victim, and that you are to be contacted personally before credit is granted.

Trade line

A trade line is an item on your credit report, referring to one of your past or present credit relationships. Trade lines normally include credit cards, mortgages, leases, and other loans. You'll have a separate trade line for each account or credit card number, whether open or closed. (Rent and utilities are not normally listed as trade lines, unless they are in collection.)

Trans Union

Trans Union is one of the three nationwide credit reporting agencies. It is headquartered in Chester, Pennsylvania and employs 3,600 people in more than 24 countries. It is a privately held corporation.

Coming Soon!!
Boss XL Media and The Agard Financial Foundation Present

- Financially Surviving COVID19 (Finding Gems in the Real Estate Market) by Carl Agard

- Financially Surviving COVID19 (Rebranding Your Business during the Pandemic) by Carl Agard

Order your copies now
www.theagardfinancialfoundation.org
Email –
agardfinancialfoundation@gmail.com

Made in the USA
Monee, IL
04 November 2026

67379797R00036